Principles of
GOOD
PARENTING

A handbook for bringing up
mentally healthy and happy children

LOUISE K. ISCOE

AC
GC
PRESS
AUSTIN CHILD GUIDANCE CENTER

Principles of Good Parenting: A Handbook for Bringing Up
Mentally Healthy and Happy Children

Copyright © 2003 by the Austin Child Guidance Center

All Rights Reserved.
No part of this book may be reproduced or utilized in any form
or by any means, electronic or mechanical, including
photocopying, recording or by any information
storage and retrieval system, without permission
in writing from the Publisher.

Inquiries should be addressed to
Austin Child Guidance Center
810 West 45th Street
Austin, Texas 78751

Iscoe, Louise K.
Principles of Good Parenting:

    p.   cm.

1. Parenting—psychology. 2. Child rearing. 3. Parental influences.
4. Parent and child. Emotional maturity. 6. Social rearing.
7. Parenting—psychological aspects.
I. Title II. Author. III Parenting. IV. Monograph.

ISBN 0-9725666-0-0

HQ 755.837L 2002   649.1Le   2002117612

2 3 4 5 6 7 8   08 07 06 05 04 03

Printed in the United States of America
at Morgan Printing in Austin, Texas

Contents

Preface 7

Introduction 11

The Importance of Mental Health 15

Becoming a Better Parent 20

Recognizing Individual Differences 23

Understanding Child Development 27

Building Good Parent/Child Relationships 31

Teaching by Example 36

Communicating with Our Children 39

Picking Our Battles 41

Getting Reassurance and Help 45

Developing Mentally Healthy Children 49

Giving and Receiving Love 52

Building Attachments 62

Enjoying Life 72

Expressing Emotions 80

Solving Problems and Tolerating Frustration 90

Getting Help 99

Conclusion 101

A Parent's Reminder 103

Contributors

This book is based on interviews conducted with members of the staff and board of the Austin Child Guidance Center, who gave freely of their knowledge, thoughts, and suggestions to help parents in rearing mentally healthy children.

Staff

Rebecca Calhoun, MA, LPC
Beth Dennis, LMSW-ACP, LMFT
Annie Dorman. MEd, LPC
Mike Hastie, LMSW-ACP, LMFT
Paula Hern, LMSW-ACP
Ana Irizarry, MA, LPC, LMFT
Nilima Mehta, MD
Linda Melnick, LMSW-ACP, LMFT
Nina Muse, MD
Anne Nelson, PhD, LMFT
Donna Reaves, MA, LPC
Elizabeth Sylvester, PhD

Key to Licensure: LPC=Licensed Professional Counselor;
LMSW-ACP=Licensed Master Social Worker-Advanced Clinical Practitioner;
LMFT=Licensed Marriage and Family Therapist

Board

Sonja Berry, LMSW-ACP
Joan Burnham, PhD
George Brown, MSW
Kira Carey, MD
Ira Iscoe, PhD
Beth Marsh
Robert Morris, LMSW
Phyllis Nelson, LMSW-ACP
Phyllis Richards, PhD
Valerie Rutledge, LMSW
David Springer, PhD

A special thanks to the Tocker Foundation
for their financial support of the printing
of this publication.

Art Director: Beth Fowler
Production Supervisor: Cinqué Hicks
Production Artists: Stephen Bright and Blake Mitchell
Text Supervisor: June Martinez
Proofreader: Misty Fisher

Preface

Bringing up children is a daunting task, often stressful and sometimes overwhelming. As parents and caregivers, we have concerns about doing the right thing or doing the wrong thing. With preschoolers there are concerns about their mental and physical development; with school-age children, worries ranging from reading problems to socializing to violence. At times the list seems almost endless.

How can parents learn how to handle the many problems that arise in rearing children?

No one can be aware of how to deal with every problem that arises or know all the right things to say and do. Where can we find the best answers?

There are, of course, a multitude of books, articles, and newspaper columns by professionals in various fields that deal with the many aspects of child rearing. A large number focus on pathology, often referred to as the mental illness or deficit model. A smaller number focus on positive mental health. This book follows the positive approach, emphasizing good coping skills and an increased ability to deal with life's challenges, whatever they may be.

This is in keeping with the goals of the Austin Child Guidance Center (ACGC), which has been serving the city of Austin and surrounding areas for more than 50 years. Its mission is to improve the mental health of children and their families through early intervention, diagnosis, and treatment to develop the emotional, behavioral, and social skills for living in an increasingly complex world. Its staff is composed of a multidisciplinary team of psychiatrists, psychologists, social workers, and counselors who provide individual, family, and group therapy; psychiatric and psychological evaluations; outdoor experiential activities; parent education; and training for current and future mental health professionals. They also offer mental health and education services to children and families in a number of community projects dealing with problems ranging from substance abuse to family violence, divorcing parents to juvenile justice.

The book is based on interviews conducted with staff and board members of the Austin Child Guidance Center. Staff are experienced in helping children and their families deal with problems large and small; board members are knowledgeable about child and family needs as well as making services available for them throughout the community. The author, who spent many hours interviewing these persons, has for many years conducted research and written articles and booklets about children from infancy to adulthood. We thank all of these men and women for giving so freely of their time, their knowledge, and their suggestions. Their contributions have resulted in a book that emphasizes some of the time-tested principles that help children cope competently in each stage of development, leading to enhanced learning abilities, resiliency, and social and personal growth and happiness for themselves and their parents.

Donald J. Zappone, DrPH
Executive Director
Austin Child Guidance Center

Introduction

Who says parenting is easy? Don't let them kid you. It is frustrating, time consuming, exhausting, challenging, sometimes frightening, always different, full of the unexpected, and never ending. It is also exciting, rewarding, and wonderful, and, arguably, the most important job we'll ever have.

Yet, most of us never receive any formal training for being a parent. Many of us don't even receive much encouragement. If we're lucky, we have family and friends to guide us, and sometimes a caring physician. If we're readers, we have books. Many of today's grandparent generation relied on Dr. Spock for everything from how to lower a fever to handling thumb sucking to concerns about a child who seemed slow to walk or talk. Today's parents have access to a number of useful books, many of them available from public libraries. Most of these are "how to" books in the sense that they explain how to deal with specific problems and concerns, and many are helpful.

This book is a bit different. First of all, it is short. As a busy parent, and perhaps one employed outside the home, you don't have much reading time. Furthermore, you're not likely to be interested in a lengthy treatise that tells you more than you want to know about a particular subject but prefer just enough to help you through a difficult time or reassure you that you're doing the right thing.

Second, it's not a how-to book. Rather, it contains suggestions and strategies to help you bring up a mentally healthy and happy child. That doesn't mean a perfect child. Rather, it means a child who is loving and caring, one who can handle frustration and make good decisions, one who can have fun and enjoy life, one who can understand and appropriately express his or her emotions. And it also contains tips to help you be a mentally healthy and happy parent.

The thoughts and suggestions in this book are from people who are knowledgeable about primary emotions and familiar with ways we can help our children identify and express them, who know the importance of tolerating frustration and who know how to teach our children about delaying gratification. They are persons who understand the importance of forming attachments to others and are experienced in making this happen, who recognize the importance of play and are practiced in helping children develop a sense of fun and an enjoyment of new experiences.

The folks whose ideas and suggestions fill the pages of this book are the staff and board members of the Austin Child Guidance Center. The staff works with children who may need a little support as they grapple with minor problems as well as those who are facing major crises or troubles of long standing. Many of them, and many of the board members, are also parents. They understand all too well that parents aren't perfect, that sometimes a parent wishes he or she could take back some ugly words or change some inappropriate actions. But they also understand that, on the whole, loving parents do their best and that, sometimes unsure, they would like guidance in how to help their youngsters grow into upstanding, competent, emotionally healthy adults.

"Emotional development," notes Stanley Greenspan, MD, in *Building Healthy Minds*,[1] "is not just the foundation for important capacities such as intimacy and trust; it is also the foundation of intelligence and a wide variety of cognitive skills. At each step of development, emotions lead the way, and learning facts and skills follow."

---

[1] Greenspan, Stanley. M.D. with Breslau Lewis, Nancy. *Building Healthy Minds: The Six Experiences that Create Emotional Growth in Babies and Young Children.* Perseus Publishing

The Importance of Mental Health

For as long as we can remember—at least since the middle of the last century—parents have been concerned about bringing up mentally healthy children who will grow into competent, happy, and productive adults. In past years, mental health simply meant the absence of mental illness. Today, the definition of positive mental health for children has been expanded to include such factors as success in school, good family relations, having friends, dealing with frustration, and, in general, successfully navigating the stages of life from infancy and early childhood through adolescence and young adulthood.

Does this mean that a mentally healthy child is one who excels in school or stars on the football team? Is it a child who never does anything wrong? Of course not. Such youngsters may or may not be mentally healthy. In fact, there is no one trait or ability that defines a child as mentally healthy. Rather, a mentally healthy child could be defined as one who exhibits a combination of social and emotional characteristics and skills including, at least to some degree, many of the following:

- A strong sense of self

- A good sense of humor

- Ability to solve problems

- Good social skills

- Good coping skills

- Curiosity about the world

- Resiliency

- Ability to enjoy new experiences

- Ability to tolerate frustration

- Ability to express and handle feelings

Mentally healthy parents also exhibit a number of characteristics and skills, among them the following:

- Are neither too rigid nor too permissive
- Allow children to express their feelings in an appropriate way
- Really listen to their children
- Treat each of their children fairly
- Allow children to problem solve when facing an obstacle
- Model healthy behavior
- Tell children what they can and cannot do
- Give choices to their children
- Are consistent in setting limits
- Are familiar with age- and developmentally appropriate behavior
- Provide a safe environment; do not allow harm to self, others, or property
- Acknowledge when they need help and know how to obtain it

- Understand that, as a child grows older, his world will gradually expand

There is more. Many parents are not aware that for children to make the transition from early childhood to "real" school—that is, kindergarten and on through the grades—they must be ready not only intellectually but also socially and emotionally. According to a national study, "research has now confirmed: Social and emotional school readiness is critical to a successful kindergarten transition, early school success, and even later accomplishments in the workplace."[2] The study goes on to say that a child who is emotionally ready for school, who possesses these attributes of good mental health, is "confident, friendly, has developed or will be able to develop good relationships with peers, and is able to concentrate on and persist at challenging tasks. The child must also be able to effectively communicate frustrations, anger, and joy and must be able to listen to instructions and be attentive."

---

[2] FANK: The Child Mental Health Foundations and Agencies Network. *A Good Beginning: Sending America's Children to School with the Social and Emotional Competence They Need to Succeed.* (Monograph) Bethesda, MD: The National Institute of Mental Health.

That said, how do we, busy parents who are immersed in many activities both in and out of our homes, manage to become the kinds of parents who will help our youngsters become emotionally healthy and happy at each stage of their lives?

Becoming a Better Parent

It has often been said that the one job for which we receive almost no training is how to be a good parent. In fact, for most of us, it is "on-the-job training," and, as is the case with almost all skills and abilities, it requires a lot of work. This book is not a training manual, and it doesn't provide answers to the many questions parents have. However, it offers some suggestions and insights that should help us become better parents.

First of all, there are many ways to be a good parent. There is no one method of good parenting, no single style that must be followed to rear healthy, well-adjusted, and happy children. Just as people differ in personality and temperament, so do their parenting styles. Some parents are soft-spoken, some loud; some delight in reading to their children while others prefer playing ball or creating art projects or roughhousing with theirs. Parents vary in the ways they show love, running the gamut from highly nurturing to tough love. They vary in the ways they show attention to their children, use humor in situations, interact with their spouse or other adults. Some are more comfortable with infants, some with older children; some are more comfortable with lively children, others with more placid ones.

As long as parents and their children are comfortable with their own family's style, these differences are unimportant. What is important is that we parents give our children unconditional love, that we respect them and value them as individuals, and that we provide them with the safety and support they need to grow into well-adjusted and emotionally healthy adults.

But it is not that simple. Beyond the child's innate tendencies and the parents' skills, there is an enormously complex interaction between parents and their children. This is further complicated by such possible realities as the absence of one or both parents, the disability of a sibling, a parent's loss of a job, and a host of other factors. Furthermore, not all of a child's characteristics or abilities are due to the family. Environment, temperament, and contacts outside the family also play a role. So what is a parent to do?

Recognizing Individual Differences

We are lucky about one thing: children don't break. Try as we might, none of us moms and dads have done everything right with our children, and no doubt occasionally we have said or done something totally wrong. Luckily, most kids turn out OK anyway. If we don't do everything right, it doesn't mean our children will be irreparably damaged. That is because children, in general, are resilient. They are born with certain traits. Some are more socially competent than others, some are more endearing and better able to attract other children and adults and get their support. Some seem to have an inborn sense of hope, a positive outlook on life; others seem fearful or moody. Some are born with an empathy for others, while some seem concerned only with themselves. Almost everyone who has more than one child has noticed that almost from the beginning their children have different temperaments.

The father of two grown daughters remembers how his children differed as 6-month-old babies. The first one, he said, would coo and smile when he would hand her a rattle and play happily with the toy. But not the second baby. She would grab the rattle with one hand, then cry and reach for more. "Throughout their childhood, our first daughter was a calm, loving child while her sister was aggressive and demanding. They've both grown into lovely young women, but their different traits were obvious from the beginning."

Sometimes, rather than treating our children as individuals, a parent will comment that "He's just like Uncle Jack," or "Cousin Mary used to sneak out of the house that way." But attributing negative qualities to a child is unfair and unreasonable. First of all, the child is himself, not his uncle Jack or her cousin

Mary. Second, too often such negative attributions become self-fulfilling prophesies. The child unconsciously—or perhaps consciously—decides that, since he's going to be compared to his scalawag uncle or sneaky aunt, he might as well behave that way.

Children vary in their genetic makeup. Scientists have long understood the genetic bearing on such things as eye color, growth patterns, and certain illnesses, but now in addition they are discovering genes that play an important part in the development of certain personality characteristics. It helps to recognize these individual differences in children, to understand that children are wired differently. Just as they look different from one another, they may respond to situations differently. Some have sunnier dispositions; some are more independent or shyer or more aggressive. The same is true of parents. Adults have different personalities and attitudes, different beliefs and feelings that effect their behavior as parents. If we are honest, we will recognize that we tend to relate better to some children than to others, to understand them better or respond more positively to them.

Biology isn't destiny. Our outlook and attitudes aren't set in concrete. Everyone can learn and change.

A renowned psychologist, Kurt Lewin, explained this through a formula: B = (P,E)—behavior equals personality plus environment. In other words, the behavior of a child is made up of the interaction of the child's personality and his physical and psychological environment, each acting upon the other and resulting in change.

Understanding
Child Development

Have you ever taken a couple of children, say a five-year-old and a nine-year-old, to play putt-putt golf? The five-year-old probably got bored after a while and just ran around hitting balls rather than playing by the rules. The nine-year-old, on the other hand, probably announced that rules are important and accused the younger child of not playing fair. It is likely that the younger child wasn't being disruptive so much as acting where she was developmentally, just as the nine-year-old, being at an age that tends to be concerned about rules, also was acting appropriately for his developmental level.

Children don't come with road maps, but there are charts on child development. While no two children are exactly alike, they generally do things in the same developmental order. We should be aware, however, that normal, healthy children may reach these stages at different times. Your baby may have started walking at 9 months, your neighbor's at 16 months. Your daughter may have been talking in sentences when she was barely two while your son at that age was saying only a word or two, and even those few words may have been difficult to understand. This doesn't mean that one child is better or brighter than the other, only that they are doing things according to their own time line, for each of these youngsters is in the normal range of development.

All children go through certain developmental stages, some more difficult to deal with than others. If we understand and accept this, it is easier on everyone. Expectations also effect how we react to our children. It is perfectly normal, for example, to regress at certain stages. A six-year-old might start clinging to mommy after months of being oh, so independent, or a three-year-old might demand a bottle when she sees her baby sister drinking from one. Development doesn't progress smoothly; there are usually bumps along the way. There is nothing to be gained by struggling over these regressions or being unduly critical of them. It is better to try to understand our child, to accept him, and to take his going back and forth in stride. It is easier on us as parents, as well as on our children, if we recognize normal development patterns. If we understand child development, we are better able to guide our children where they are developmentally, which not only helps but also saves us a lot of worry, as well.

We sometimes forget that emotional development is not always in sync with physical development. Children function at the stage where they are. Look, for example, at your pre-teen and her friends. Around age 12, children develop a new self-awareness as social creatures. A teenage boy may suddenly wear his feelings on his sleeves, blubbering if teased, while a girl that age may feel left out by other girls or think she is not as attractive as the others. Telling a boy not to cry or a girl that you think she is pretty doesn't make a difference. They need time and a safe place to work things out. As children grow older and become more independent, we parents may have an illusion of control, but we can't direct our children any more. What we can do is continue to listen to them, give them time, and guide them in appropriate behavior to help them grow through their adolescence and into mentally healthy adults. We are all happier if we give our children space, if we are joyful for them without wanting to change them.

Most of us want and expect our children to grow through normal developmental stages. If we are unfamiliar with these stages, reference books at libraries or bookstores provide information that can be useful and reassuring. A knowledge of child development helps us better understand our youngsters and have more realistic expectations of their abilities and behavior. But for parents who have concerns, it makes sense to question family or friends, to talk to and get advice from them, to have our thoughts and feelings validated. If there is real cause for concern, it is wise to check with a professional. Too often, parents feel that they have done something wrong if their children don't seem to be growing or progressing as they think they should. More than likely, the problem is not the fault of a parent. And it is also more than likely that some professional counseling may help a child become more comfortable with and understanding of himself, in turn making the parents happier, as well.

Building Good Parent/Child Relationships

It helps to be aware of some of the things that hinder good parent-child relationships and that can be avoided once we are aware of them. One is ego-involvement. For example, how would you answer this question: "If my child has a tantrum, will people think I'm a bad mother?" How often do we worry that if our child does something inappropriate, or doesn't do something well, others will consider it a reflection on us as parents? Or, if our child sings well or hits a home run, do we think it will reflect well on us as parents?

It is easy to fall into that way of thinking, to have an illusion of control. That is, if our child does well, we consider it to our credit, but if he does poorly, we see it as our fault. Forget it. Let's not focus on ourselves but on our children. Remember that my child is not me, your child is not you. We can try to do our best as parents, but our children are unique human beings. They have our genes and they learn from us, but they are not reflections of ourselves.

We parents don't fail when our children don't turn out as we had hoped or envisioned. Rather, we fail when our own needs supplant the needs of our children. As parents, we do of course have some practical needs. These might be, say, to get the kids up at 7, prepare school lunches, get the children to day care or school, get to work on time, and all the other elements of family routine. But a parent's emotional needs are something else. Parents who praise their children only when they win a Little League game or take honors in a tiny tot beauty contest are letting their own needs come before those of their children. We don't want others to treat us that way, and we shouldn't treat our kids that way. When a child strikes out or is on the losing team is when he needs parental support most. Parental needs also intrude when a father or mother yells at the umpire, blaming him for a bad call against his or her child. It might be tempting, but think of the kind of behavior we model for our children when we are rude or blame others for what our youngster has or hasn't done.

Being a parent is a hard and often unappreciated job. Each day, we don't know whether we are succeeding; it is an ongoing test. Most parents want to do a good job rearing their children and to change if what they're doing doesn't seem to be working. But change is difficult. It is far easier to do what is familiar even if it is not quite the right thing to do. Sometimes adults who want to be better parents than their own parents had been may defend their parents' aberrant behavior, claiming, for example, that "My father hit me when I was a child because I needed it, and I turned out OK, so it's OK to hit my child." No matter how hard we try, we all slip occasionally, especially if a particular behavior hits a sore spot from our own childhood.

However, hitting or yelling or other forms of aggression rarely bring about the desired results. Down deep, most of us realize that it would be better to try something else. To be better parents, we should be open to recognizing how we might change, how we might learn new techniques. We should be open to trying something new and then, if that doesn't work, trying something else. Sometimes an approach works for awhile, but as the child develops it loses its impact. That doesn't mean we have done something wrong. Rather, it means that as our child grows, something else is called for to help him along.

People don't seek or like change. A hopeful sign is when a parent is willing to acknowledge she needs help, to try to change her behavior out of concern for her child's development. But take note: when parents change, their children may not improve for some time. In fact, they may actually act worse for awhile. That can be discouraging. It is easy to give up if our efforts seem useless. Nonetheless, it is important to hang in there. We have to go on blind faith that our children's behavior and attitude will improve in time. It is like a dance: if one stops, the other can't continue the same dance alone—and thus, in time, change occurs.

There are no absolute answers when it comes to rearing emotionally healthy children, and no guarantees. We are all going to make mistakes. Furthermore, there is no single way to bring up mentally healthy children. What works with one child at one time may not work at another time, and it may not work with another child. The important thing is to be honest with ourselves, to recognize if we should be doing something differently, and to be willing to learn and change.

Teaching by Example

The primary way we teach our children is not by what we tell them but by the example we set. The old adage, "actions speak louder than words," is one way of saying it; "role modeling" is another. As parents, it is how we act or respond in various situations—how we treat other people, how we handle anger or unhappiness, how we follow through on things that we said we would do, and whether our words and our actions are in accord with one another—that show our children how adults act and, in turn, model how they should act. If we demonstrate acceptance of other people and other ideas, we teach our children to be accepting. If we apologize to our children when we've been impatient or unkind, they will be more likely to recognize when they have hurt another child or adult and apologize to them. If we don't want our children to speak unkindly of others, to swear, to badmouth their teachers, we shouldn't talk to them in those ways. Children may talk and act differently among themselves than when they are with adults, but our examples are what provide the foundation in which they develop and grow in their relationships to individuals and groups.

As parents, we also model our faith. This may be an organized faith, such as a traditional religion, or a more individual faith. Whatever its form, faith provides children a way in which to view the world and their place in it, a way to develop a sense of values and trust and hope. Faith provides a way for children to carry through in difficult times, to deal with adversity, to persist despite setbacks, to develop positive values. The examples parents set by adhering to a positive belief system can help our children develop a life-enhancing faith. This, in turn, can help nurture positive mental health.

Parents aren't perfect, but we should try to act with as much grace as we can muster. After all, everyone makes mistakes. It is as important for children to see how their parents deal with shame or mistakes as it is to see how they handle having fun, getting an award, or cleaning the house. It is important for our children to see us taking responsibility for our own actions and how our trust and our faith help us weather some of our most trying and difficult times. Role modeling is something that starts early and builds a foundation for how our children will view others and the world around them as well as how they will act themselves.

Communicating with Our Children

The main way we communicate with adults is by talking to them. But apart from telling our children what or what not to do, do we talk with them? Do we listen to and hear them? It is important for us to talk to our children. It is even more important to listen to them. By keeping the lines of communication open, we are more likely to be able to talk and listen to our children as they reach the teen years, and they will be more likely to talk and listen to us. In turn, we will be better able to give, and they to accept, the support and encouragement that they will continue to need. When we don't talk to one another, when we keep things bottled up inside, problems fester. How often has someone said, "I wish I'd told her," about some unresolved issue before it was too late.

Take time to listen. Sometimes it is better to stop doing the laundry and focus on the kids. Talk to children as if they were intelligent, because they probably are. Help them find answers rather than giving them answers. You might say, "'Let's talk about that. What would happen if you did that?'" Parents can help children think through an issue, help them recognize that actions have consequences, some good and some not.

Sometimes we have to work consciously to develop the ability to talk to one another, to express our feelings in words. Things don't always work out smoothly, but if we make the effort to communicate, we at least give better relationships a chance.

Parents and caregivers also need to communicate with one another. Although no two persons consistently handle things the same way, a mother and father—or parent and caregiver, grandparents, or whoever is rearing a child—will be more effective in guiding their children if they are in sync with one another and are able to present a united front, and they give their kids less opportunity to play one adult against the other. It is better for our kids as well as for us, their parents and caregivers.

Picking Our Battles

As parents, we sometimes have an illusion of control over our children. When control is for safety—to stop a child from running out in the street, for example, or from putting his hand on a hot stove —it is good. But too many things become control issues that have no impact on safety, things that escalate into power struggles and battles. These not only don't help, but also, when carried to extremes can do a great deal of harm to a family.

Parents and experts agree: the best approach is to pick your battles. Most things are negotiable with children. It doesn't help if we regress to our youngster's level. A young man told a story that illustrated this point. "I was putting my five-year-old nephew to bed one night," he said, "and after a story and a hug, I turned out the light. 'I want the light on,' my nephew said. I explained that it was easier to go to sleep when it was dark, and left the light off. When I passed by his room a few minutes later, I noticed that the light was on. We went through this several times: I turned the light out, and as soon as I left, he turned it on. Finally, in frustration and determined to be in charge, I unscrewed the light bulb and took it out of the room. And next thing I knew he had turned on the closet light. So I did what I should have done in the beginning," he continued. "I suggested to my nephew that I could turn on the hall light and leave his bedroom door open. That way, light would shine in his room but the bedroom light would be off. And you know, with that compromise we both saved face and were content."

Potential battles come in all shapes and sizes, and most aren't worth it. A mother gave another example. When her daughter was about four, she loved coloring on her bedroom walls. At first, the mother kept scolding her. After thinking it over and realizing that no one would be hurt, no matter what color the child's room was, the mother changed her approach. "I'll tell you what," she suggested. "Let's paint your room, and I'll help if you'd like. What color would you like me to use?" This led to some good times for the woman and her little girl, if to rather unusual decor. Every now and then the child, with her mother's agreement and sometimes her help, painted different things on the walls—animals, star wars, whatever she liked. Then one day when she was about 11, she asked her mother "would be OK if I paint my room one color so it will look more grown up when I have friends over?" The mother just smiled and told her it would be fine. It took a lot of patience on her part, but neither safety nor ethics were issues so it didn't really matter.

Meal time tends to become a battleground in families. Most kids won't starve themselves intentionally. If they don't like or want to eat one meal, they probably will eat at the next. If we serve something they really don't like, it helps to have something nourishing that they like on the table such as peanut butter, carrot sticks, or pasta. We shouldn't take it personally if they don't like the food we serve. It is neither a personal offense nor a reflection on our cooking. The main thing is, be reasonable. Don't let food become an issue. Battles over food not only spoil mealtime but also too often lead to later problems.

Sometimes unconsciously we set our children up for failure. Let's say we want to teach our youngster to be responsible, so we suggest it will be his task to take out the trash each week. But we also don't want spills. Let's be realistic. We probably can't have it both ways with a young child. Either we should accept a few spills or find another chore that he could handle more competently as well as responsibly.

Negotiating options is an effective way to avoid battles. In this way no one has to win or lose. Proving dominance is an empty victory. That is good to remember when our teenager dyes her hair green or wears unmatched socks. Small acts of rebellion may be hard on parents, but, if they don't interfere with school work or safety or anything else of importance, why make an issue of them? It is more important to focus on staying in school than on a hair color that is probably only temporary. In most cases, if it is not a safety issue, there is no need for a long discussion. That is a good rule to help us pick our battles. It avoids much unnecessary conflict.

Getting Reassurance and Help

At times almost all parents need a little help, and we shouldn't hesitate to get it. Luckily there are tools to help us. One is to learn informally by sharing experiences with friends or family. How often has a mother said to a friend, "You mean your child does that too?" It is reassuring to learn that other little boys wet the bed occasionally or that little girls sometimes won't let others play with their toys. It is helpful to learn from other mothers how they handled a given situation, or how, sometimes, the situation resolved itself in time.

Another is to make use of information available free from public libraries, schools, health clinics, churches, and the internet. Books and articles are good resources as guides, though they may not provide solutions to our particular problems. Some of us might be embarrassed to admit that we need help or guidance, or we may lack the confidence to seek it. But seeking help doesn't mean we're not smart. On the contrary, it means we are smart enough to know that we need something to help our children and that we are confident that we can find it and use it.

With the decrease in family size and the increase in family mobility in the past quarter century, today's parents and children often lack the support and encouragement of the extended family. Time was when grandparents and cousins and aunts and uncles played an important role in helping young parents, giving them reassurance, suggestions, and a different perspective as well as providing baby sitting and other welcome services. Few of us are lucky enough to have family nearby today. This makes it especially important for parents to maintain relationships with adults outside the family. In place of distant family, parents' good friends can become an important part of a child's life.

Parents often feel isolated. Many new mothers find it helpful to join a group such as parents of newborns or an exercise group. Hospital maternity wards often provide information on groups of this type, as do public libraries, churches, and well-baby clinics. Being with other new mothers helps us realize that we are all in the same boat. We might meet other parents at the park, at school, or at church. By spending time with people who have children the same ages as our own, we can be reassured that what our child is doing is normal, find out how others handle similar situations, or perhaps learn that our youngster needs some help. In addition to the sociability, the support of other parents helps us realize that we are not alone.

As parents, we are often insecure in our judgments about rearing our children. After all, we figure, experts have been trained in working with children and therefore must know more than we do. Often we don't recognize our own capabilities. Experts have useful information and skills, and they can be extremely helpful. Parents, however, have experiential knowledge; we have our children's best interest at heart. We are our children's primary teachers.

How does a parent know when to seek professional guidance? Often it is when we are concerned beyond the normal worries that go with child rearing. It might be when we are worried about our child's physical or mental development, behavior, or a problem that seems beyond our ability to deal with effectively. Seeking help doesn't mean we are bad parents. On the contrary, it shows that we are concerned enough about our children to find ways to do the best we can for them. Some suggestions for obtaining professional guidance are given later in this book.

Developing Mentally Healthy Children

Among the many duties and pleasures of child rearing is teaching. We may not be professional teachers, but from the time we show our infants how to hold a cup and eat with a spoon, our preschooler how to tie or velcro his shoes, our teenager how to drive a car, we are teaching our children the skills and abilities that will enable them to get along in the world.

But there are other things that we teach that go beyond how to perform a task or develop a skill. These are the qualities and characteristics that are essential for children to develop to become emotionally healthy adults. We don't teach these by showing a small child how to build a block tower or ride a tricycle or a sixth-grader how to solve a math problem. Rather, we teach these qualities by modeling them, by the way we act with our children and families and friends, by the way we guide our children in developing into caring, responsive, respectful, and competent human beings. These qualities must be taught, or modeled, over and over again as children develop. Often, we are not even aware we are teaching them or that our children are observing and learning from our actions.

Studies have shown that good mental health is based on a solid social and emotional foundation. It cannot be taught or acquired in one day but is developed from infancy onward. As studies have shown, "Children who have close relationships with responsive parents (or a consistent caregiver) early in life are able to develop healthy relationships with peers as they get older. An early relationship with a responsive parent also serves as a 'security blanket' for children, allowing them to feel more secure in exploring and mastering the outside world. Parents who talk with and respond to their children also make them feel as if they have some control over their own environment, boosting their self-esteem."[3]

Although many qualities might be considered important in rearing emotionally healthy children, five seem essential. Without them, a person might muddle through life adequately. With them, a child has the best chance of growing into a mentally and emotionally healthy adult. These qualities, or abilities, are:

- Giving and receiving love

- Building attachments

- Enjoying life

- Expressing emotions

- Solving problems and handling frustration

Following is an explanation of these qualities, along with some suggestions to help us, as parents and caregivers, develop them in our children.

---

[3] FANK: The Child Mental Health Foundations and Agencies Network. *A Good Beginning: Sending America's Children to School with the Social and Emotional Competence They Need to Succeed.* (Monograph) Bethesda, MD: The National Institute of Mental Health.

Giving and Receiving Love

Unconditional love! We seek it at every age. For children, the most important thing is to know they are loved. Our children won't know that unless we show them and tell them in many different ways how much we love them. The one thing that should be consistent in our children's lives is their parents' love.

Why is love important? After all, you may know some adults who grew up emotionally healthy despite not having a loving family. Perhaps they had someone positive in their lives, a grandparent, for example, or a neighbor, minister, or family friend who loved them, making up for the love that they lacked at home. Perhaps they had inborn traits that enabled them to overcome neglect or abuse. And perhaps they might have been happier or more productive had their families been more loving, but still they were able to muddle through and build a satisfactory life. Although some children "make it" without love, some don't, and many more are caught in the middle, doing all right but aware that life for them could have been better. When nobody cares about a child, she can't establish loving relationships. There may be academic discussions about the value of nature vs. nurture, but in real life a child needs both.

Love is one of the most fundamental human behaviors, and in many ways it is basic to emotional health. The giving of love encompasses a wide variety of attributes including respect, tolerance, closeness, understanding, and trust.

How do we show love?

- Cuddling a sleepy baby, holding our arms out to a toddler taking his first steps, waving encouragingly to a five-year-old as she heads for her first day of kindergarten, and praising a ten-year-old for his improvement in arithmetic are all signs of love. Being kind to animals, showing concern for other people's children, and caring for friends and neighbors are ways in which parents model love and set the stage for their children's ability to give love. Small ways, all, but showing love in small ways many times a day is so important in a child's life.

- Being available. Being attentive. Being consistent.

- Reinforcing the fact that we care. Give a lot of hugs to children of all ages. Some parents are afraid that outward displays of affection will make them look weak. Sometimes we are just too tired. It takes time and energy, emotional as well as physical energy, when we come home tired and really would like a little time to ourselves, but our kids don't think about that. They want to see us when we walk in the door, and they want us to reassure them that we love them. Kids need hugs. They need love reinforced.

- Expressing love verbally. Just as we, as adults, like to hear words of love, so do our children. It isn't enough to say, "She knows I love her." Have you told her so recently? If we want our children to be loving and caring, perhaps we should first look at ourselves. It is hard for some people to express their feelings. They are uncomfortable telling a child that they love him, perhaps commenting that when they were growing up their family didn't think it was appropriate or manly to express emotions. Well, we are adults now, and we should try to get over our discomfort or lack of experience in the interest of helping our children. In the process, we may find that it is easier than we thought and that it makes us feel good, as well. We can't say "I love you" just once to a child and expect it to suffice any more than we can to an adult.

- Doing the difficult things. Love is not about gifts and flowers; it is day in and day out; it is honest. Showing love is an ongoing process. It requires perseverance, respect, patience, and grace. Love is about helping our children feel good about themselves. From our baby's infancy through toddler hood through the school and teenage years, we should try to help our children feel taller in our presence.

- Meaning what we say and do. As the old axiom says, it's not so much what you do as how you do it; not what you say as how you say it. Sometimes our words or our feelings don't agree with our actions, and children are quick to realize this. A preschool teacher became painfully aware of this when a little girl in her class said to her, "You don't like me, do you." Taken aback, the teacher asked, "Why do you say that?" "Because you shiver when you touch me," the child replied. Children know whether their parents or caregivers love them or not. Repeating "I love you" without some accompanying emotional expression is merely an empty phrase.

How do we avoid using love as a tool? As parents, we sometimes say or do something that our children perceive as a withdrawal of our love. In other words,

- Don't use love to threaten a child. Sometimes, for example, we hear a parent say to a youngster, "I won't love you if you don't clean your room." But threats won't encourage children to do what we want. Rather, it will make them think we love them only for what they do to please us, not for themselves. We shouldn't tell our children that we will withdraw our love if they don't do what we say.

- Don't use put downs. Think how a child feels who, already upset that he has spilled the milk, hears his mother say, "You are so clumsy!" How much better he would feel if she were to suggest that he help clean up the milk and, next time, hold the pitcher in two hands.

- Don't embarrass a child. It is one thing to suggest to your daughter that she wear a different dress, another to tell her that she looks terrible.

How we help our children grow socially and emotionally is a way of showing love. As children grow, it is important to let them know we love them but we don't always love their behavior. If a toddler bites another child, for example, it is helpful to let him know that "I love you but I can't accept what you're doing." Guiding and teaching children shows them that we care. Letting them get away with negative behavior may appear loving to children at the moment, but over the long run it shows only that we didn't care enough to guide them in becoming mentally healthy and productive adults.

Setting appropriate limits, or boundaries, is a way of showing love. Parents are responsible for setting boundaries to help a child feel safe. Sometimes we are afraid to set limits, fearing that our children won't like us if we put restrictions on their activities. The important thing is to recognize the balance between adventure and safety. A two-year-old has to learn not to run out in the street; a six-year-old must be taught how to look both ways before crossing the street; a teenager must be told what time to be home at night. Limits, in other words, must be appropriate for a child's developmental level, and they must assure the child's safety. It is a parent's responsibility to prevent children from hurting themselves or others, but it is also important to recognize a child's age and ability and to be tolerant of the learning process.

Once children reach school age, a common response to parental limits is "everybody's doing it." That's the line used when preteens and teenagers want to go to a certain movie, for example, or buy a trendy pair of shoes. We have all heard it, and sometimes it is difficult not to give in. But check it out first. As one mother used to tell her kids, "I don't have a child named 'everybody.'" Some things may be OK to do, but others may not. A useful tool is to suggest, "Let me talk to your friend's mother about that." If you do, you are likely to find that everybody is not doing it, possibly that no one is doing it, or that your child backs off before you ever make that phone call. At times kids are relieved when a parent says "no" because it gets them off the hook and lets them save face by having a parent to blame. It is a given that children try to get away with things (can't you remember doing something like that?), but wise parents let their children know that they are in charge, that they are the parents and are concerned about their children's safety and welfare.

As far as our children getting angry when we set limits, forget about it. Most children will fuss about parental restrictions anyway, because that is just what kids do. That is especially true of teenagers. In some ways it is easier on parents as a child grows, in some ways more difficult. While they are small, parents are better able to keep them safe. When they are older, and drive cars or hang out with friends we don't know, we worry more. Parents have a different kind of involvement during their children's teen years, but it is every bit as important.

How often have we wondered if our children hear what we say to them? How often does it seem that what we say goes unheeded? In fact, our sons and daughters often hear us even when they don't seem to be paying attention. What we say usually sinks in even if they don't always follow our advice, but we can't be sure until much later. No matter how angry or disinterested they might seem, if we have had fairly good communication over the years, our daughters and sons will continue to hear what we say. Besides not letting them get away with inappropriate behavior, our concern shows that we care about them. When we back off at a sign of a child's or teenager's anger, our son or daughter may interpret our action as a lack of concern.

Teaching appropriate behavior, which includes setting limits and defining boundaries, means guidance, not control. What is more, it can't wait until a child is 6 or 10 or 13. Learning appropriate behavior starts when a child is very young; teaching it is a repetitive process. The message may remain the same, but it is given differently to youngsters of different ages and in different situations. By repeating the lessons we want our children to learn through modeling and speaking, and by making these life lessons developmentally appropriate, children will learn. This is another way of giving love.

Building Attachments

Just as children need nourishment to grow and develop a healthy body, they need emotional nourishment to develop good mental health. They need to feel secure and loved to be able to relate well with others, to attach or bond with their primary caregiver. Attachment is relating to others. Without basic attachment, without the ability to relate to and bond with others, they cannot develop in an emotionally healthy way.

A key to attachment, and the basis for all good relationships, is trust. Eric Ericson, a respected psychologist, has emphasized the importance of establishing basic trust as the first condition for building attachment to others. According to Ericson, a child needs to know that his environment can be trusted and that his elemental needs of infancy will be satisfied in order to bond with his caregivers. Trust grows first from a loving home environment, then from a positive association with two or three non-family members such as a relative, a neighbor, a baby sitter, or a family friend. Children develop trust early through activities with other children in a supportive and secure environment. These may be structured activities such as an early childhood program or a library story hour, or they may be informal, such as a neighborhood play group or playing in the park. Even in informal settings, however, adult supervision is important to provide a balance between developing trust and maintaining safety.

There are many ways to foster attachment and build trust, but there is no single formula. The first and most important way is to give and receive love. That is the way we help an infant begin to build attachment to others—to mom and dad, other family members, friends. Being there for our children and meeting their needs for affection, nurturance, and protection are essential ingredients. People vary in the ways they show affection. It can be physical, with hugging, body language, and facial expressions. It can be verbal, through loving words and tone of voice. And of course it can be both. As long as people are sincere and have confidence in themselves as loving parents, their children more than likely will respond to their love. But attachment is a two-way street. Early reciprocity between an infant and parent or caregiver, or being in tune with one another, is needed for a baby to establish trust.

As adults, most of us recognize the importance of loving and being loved. However, if we don't learn this in infancy and have it reinforced as we develop, we may have problems relating to others as we grow older. Attachment is experiential: we can't give it if we have never experienced it ourselves. One need only look at the recent spate of school shootings by adolescents to recognize the need for people to develop attachments to others rather than to become alienated from them. When no one cares about a child, he can't establish loving relationships. When no one values him, he won't value others.

Children learn about relationships from the way their parents and other caregivers act as much as from what they say. As parents, we model our relationships when we interact with our husbands or wives, our other children and family members, our neighbors and friends. Through our actions, our children learn how to get along with and treat people of all ages. If we don't show respect for others, how will our children learn?

We also model our acceptance of our children. For them to be able to attach to others, to love and be loved, we show our children that we love them unconditionally, that we accept them for who they are. But as anyone with more than one child realizes, children are different. An adventurous child may embrace new experiences, a fearful child back away from them. An extrovert may greet everyone he meets as a friend, an introvert shy from contact. And we, because of our own temperaments and personalities, may relate to our children differently. A child's temperament often affects the way in which his parents respond to him. Sometimes a parent's and child's temperament are a good match, while in other cases they may seem at cross purposes. It is important to recognize temperamental differences and to respect them. Comparing one child to another—asking our little boy why he can't behave as well as his sister or our daughter why she can't get good grades as a friend's daughter does—says to our children that we don't love them for who they are but for what they do, that we don't love them as much as the well-behaved child or the one with better grades. Children often go through stages of feeling unloved or unlovable despite our best intentions. As parents, we don't want them to feel that way because of something we have said or done.

We should also model that we, as adults, are trying to grow, that one keeps growing throughout life. If we have made mistakes along the way with our children—and who hasn't—it is not hopeless. It helps children to see that we are not perfect, that we are willing to acknowledge our mistakes and try to do differently and better next time. Some call this "falling forward." From our mistakes we can learn; from them, we can develop fuller relationships. On the other hand, if we don't admit that we overreacted, for example, or if we don't say we are sorry for a mistake we have made, our children won't have a model for honesty and a willingness to grow. As parents, we sometimes have a hard time acknowledging our mistakes.

Whatever their inclination, children are trainable, and we can guide them in learning the social skills that will help them get along with others. A shy child, for example, can be encouraged to look people in the eye when she is talking to them, to speak when spoken to. While we should recognize different temperaments and styles, we should also recognize that each of us must learn to get along with and negotiate with others throughout our lives. That, too, is an aspect of good mental health.

We should also help our children develop empathy, which is recognizing the feelings of others. This is a way we relate to others, the give and take of being social beings. It is the opposite of antisocial behavior. Without empathy, a person can't connect with the feelings of others. Without empathy, there is no remorse.

It may take some effort on our part to respect our child's feelings. We may mean to. Yet how often have we heard a parent say "you shouldn't feel that way" to a child who is angry at a teacher because he got a bad grade or hurt because he wasn't invited to a party. The parent's comment in effect tells a child that his feelings are wrong or unimportant, even though that probably is not what we meant. It helps children much more to acknowledge their feelings, then guide them in learning to deal with them.

We can help our children develop empathy. If two children are fighting over a toy in the sandbox, a parent might ask her child how he thinks the other child feels. "Look at his face," we might say. "How do you think he is feeling when you grab the toy from him? How do you feel when he grabs the toy from you?" Another way would be to model empathic behavior by reflecting the child's feelings. We could say, for example, "I can understand how that would hurt your feelings," then suggest an option: "You might share your bucket with Joey, and he can share his shovel with you."

One suggestion for teaching young children empathy, to help them recognize that other people have feelings, too, is to talk about what emotions look like. Using the simple happy face as an example, we might draw several round faces with different expressions from happy to sad, then, talk to our child about how people's faces look when they have different feelings. We could also talk about body language—how people slump or drag their feet if they are unhappy or how they scowl if they are angry. Sometimes it helps to diffuse a situation if we can recognize and acknowledge how another person feels. "It looks like you're having a tough day" is far more effective than telling a child to stop behaving in a negative way. How we manage our feelings can effect our health. The ability to understand others can help our children get along in school and lead healthier, happier lives.

Young children (as all of us, at times) are wrapped up in themselves, and it takes guidance for them to realize that other children have feelings, too. It is important for all of us to see others as being like ourselves, not as lesser human beings, and it is important to help our children understand this. They need to learn that sometimes each of us hurts and sometimes each of us feels good, that you are like me in many ways and I am like you. They should learn that we also are different in some ways, but that has nothing to do with value. We are no better or worse because of our differences; that is merely the way we are.

The best parenting tools are listening and time. By listening to our children in a nonjudgmental way, by giving them our undivided attention, we show them love and respect. We show them that we value them as human beings. "Being there" means being available emotionally, not just physically. It means being able to reflect back, to mirror what our child is saying. For an infant to feel loved and safe we provide physical security. For older children, providing security is being there when problems arise. Just because our adolescent children may look like young adults and seem to reject our counsel, they still need us to be there for them, to reflect their emotions back to them. This is true at every level. The key is to help them handle their feelings and emotions in a developmentally or age-appropriate way.

There are ways to make time for relating to others, time to build attachment. How about eating together? Sometimes we may have to work late or one of our kids has soccer practice, but with a little effort most parents can arrange a time to have the evening meal together. That means sitting down to dinner with the TV off. It means not limiting conversation to "eat your spinach" or "stop poking your little sister." Rather, it means turning dinner time into sharing time, a time when the children have a chance to talk about their day and parents to talk about theirs. Driving a child to a piano lesson or a dentist appointment are just a couple of other ways we can use time together as an opportunity to build and keep positive relationships.

Parents are busy people, and finding time as we rush from work to carpooling to home and the many tasks awaiting us is certainly not easy. Children of every age often want to talk at the "wrong" time— when we are fixing dinner or rushing out the door or are exhausted at the end of a long day. But the time is right for them, and we should respect that. One experience builds on another. By giving them time and attention when they need it, we can help them build the attachment and trust that will enable them to have healthy relationships as they grow and progress through life.

Enjoying Life

Play is the work of childhood, the business of children. It is how children learn. We have heard this; we have read about it. Journal articles have been written about it, and studies on brain development reinforce it. What it means is that play is a way of acting on materials and on the environment, a way of learning about the world around us.

Parents are concerned sometimes that their children aren't learning anything in preschool. They want their youngsters to learn their numbers and letters and how to read. But if you spent some time in a preschool classroom, you would find that children are not just kneading play dough or piling blocks. True, they are playing, but at the same time they are improving their motor skills as they shape the clay, increasing their language skills when talking to their playmates or the teacher, developing cognitive skills when they figure what size block to use to span a space. After watching for awhile, a parent is likely to comment that they didn't realize all that was going on, adding, "I thought they were just playing."

Adults often misunderstand how children learn at different developmental levels. Three- and four-year-olds try things out, explore, test out a new toy or experience. They find order and sequence in playing with blocks, for example, lining them up from smallest to largest. Nine- and ten-year-olds like rules. They like to play games where they follow directions, do things as they are expected to. It isn't until age 11 or 12 that youngsters start analyzing, start thinking as adults. Children think differently at different levels. None of these approaches is right or wrong. Rather, each is appropriate at a given stage of development.

What do children gain through play?

- Through play, children develop the social skills they need for life. They learn to cooperate, to get along with others, to play fair. They learn rules and how to take turns. Children express interest and concerns through play; they communicate through play. They learn some of the norms and standards of behavior that society expects of them.

- Joy in play and in both familiar and new experiences helps children experience enjoyment throughout their lives. Children enjoy playtime. Through play, they not only learn but they also experience joy. It isn't necessary or even wise to "teach" whenever we play with our children, or to use play time to meet our own needs. Sometimes, in fact, adults must teach themselves not to squelch the joy of kids. When a mom or dad is overstressed, as so many are these days, it can be difficult to feel and show enjoyment and playfulness. But it is worth making the effort.

- Play is good family time. Some of the traditional games, such as popular board games, bingo, and card games provide an opportunity for good interaction between and among children and their parents or caregivers. Video and automated games are something else. Many youngsters like them, but they fail to offer the interactive qualities of games played with people rather than with a computer. Children often have their own suggestions of games to play. Listen to them, and when possible follow their lead. People tend to relax when they play, to communicate better, to open up. When families play games at an appropriate level for the children, there is an equality that children enjoy. The child, rather than the parent, might be in charge of the checker board, for example, giving her a feeling of control and building her self-confidence. Mastering a new game, especially with the encouragement of a supportive adult, also can be confidence building.

- Playfulness, or a sense of play, can make life more enjoyable for parents and children alike. Consider a long car trip, for example. If a parent fusses at the kids and tells them how dull and boring it will be, it probably will be. But if a parent piques the children's interest, lets them help plan part of the trip, and has games to play and things to look for on the drive, it can be an adventure. Even getting ready for bed can take place in a playful mood. "I'll race you," mom might say. "Let's see who can get our pj's on first." A sense of play, a feeling of enjoyment, can make all the difference.

• Rituals are meaningful to children, and play can become a treasured ritual. Most of us at any age look forward to certain rituals—birthdays, Christmas, perhaps when the neighborhood swimming pool opens each summer or going out for pizza on the last day of school. Play also can become a ritual. Some families get up a softball game when the family gets together, others get out a jigsaw puzzle for everyone to work on. Whether the rituals come naturally, such as a holiday, or are developed within a family, they are something to which family members of all ages look forward. They are predictable; they help us feel secure. There is something reassuring and satisfying about knowing what to expect.

- An introduction to the arts provides children with another opportunity to find enjoyment in life. Music, art, and literature; plays, concerts, and dance; and sports events of all kinds open worlds to children beyond home and school. Many communities offer free or nominally priced events so most youngsters can attend. In addition to looking and listening, many children get pleasure from trying out and developing their own skills— playing an instrument in the school band, sculpting clay, singing in the choir. As parents, our job is to be an encouraging and appreciative audience. If, as teenagers, our children's tastes in music, art, or sports diverge from ours, we needn't be upset unless they prefer something bizarre or dangerous. Most will temper their tastes in time, and the enjoyment of cultural and sports events developed in childhood can last a lifetime.

There are many kinds of play—physical and intellectual, directed and nondirected, structured and unstructured, social and solitary. Since school recess has been abolished almost entirely, there is less and less time for free play. Today the trend is toward organized play. One reason for this change is that both moms and dads tend to be employed, and no one is home after school to keep an eye on the kids. Some children are told to come straight home from school and stay in the house until a parent or caregiver returns; others are in a multitude of after-school activities. In either case, free play falls by the wayside, removing one of the time-honored ways for children to learn problem solving, decision making, creativity, resourcefulness, and how to get along with others. It is our responsibility as parents to provide a balance between structured activities and free play for our children. We shouldn't underestimate their importance.

Children don't need fun to be happy, nor do they need a constant round of "fun" activities. Far more important is the ability to find enjoyment in whatever they are doing. With a positive attitude we can make everyday activities pleasurable—helping clean the house ("if you find any coins under the couch cushions or on the floor, you can keep them," a mother might say); working in the yard ("let's clear a small space for you to grow your own veggies"); taking a walk ("let's see how many different kinds of flowers or bugs we can see"). Many children today grow up thinking they must be entertained. How much healthier it is to help them build in an attitude that life, with all its wonders, is to be enjoyed. Entertainment and fun are short-lived. The ability to find pleasure and enjoyment in whatever one does is with a child for the rest of his life.

Expressing Emotions

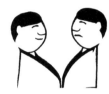

We all have feelings, and we all express them in some way. But sometimes we forget that our children's feelings are as meaningful to them as our own are to us.

How often have we, as parents, unthinkingly denied our child's feelings. "You shouldn't be jealous of your baby brother," we might say, adding, "No, you can't put him in the garbage can." Annoyed as we might be, wouldn't it show more understanding to say something like, "It's really hard having a baby around, isn't it? He needs so much attention, and he's not big enough to play with you. Now, why don't you build something with blocks so I can watch you while I feed the baby, then we'll go outside and I'll push you on the swing." In other words, accept the child's feelings but divert them into a positive channel.

The same approach is helpful when a child tells a parent that she is afraid or hurt or angry. We can validate her feelings by telling her that it is all right to feel that way, then help her figure out how to deal with the problem and the feelings. This approach helps children recognize that if they are of value, their feelings are of value. At the same time it helps them learn to work through their problems and feelings, to manage their feelings in a positive way.

If a child devotes his energy to holding his emotions in, he won't have energy for other things. It is not healthy for a child to keep everything bottled up inside or to take out his anger in inappropriate or destructive ways. A child who is mad at mom and can't express his feelings may take out his anger by bullying other children; a child, who is picked on at school but can't talk to his parents about it, may show his frustration by doing poorly in school. It is up to us, as parents, to help our children find appropriate ways to express their emotions.

Such feelings and consequent actions affect future successes. In social situations and in the work world, young people and adults who haven't learned how to express and handle their emotions in appropriate ways are likely to have trouble in school, in their jobs, and in their personal relationships. In fact, the two greatest detriments to mental health are anger and anxiety. Research has shown that anger interferes with the ability to consider other behavioral options, while anxiety leads to insecurity and inhibits the development of coping skills and abstract thinking.

As parents, we sometimes need tools to help our children handle their feelings. What emotions is the child expressing? Is the child expressing his feelings by acting out, crying, screaming, hiding from the situation, being aggressive, retreating, or some combination of these behaviors? The ways in which a child is expressing his feelings at the moment are probably the only way he knows to deal with them. Some children lose their cool more easily than others; some get hurt easily while others are quick to anger. We need to let children know that it's OK to have feelings, OK to be angry, but it is important to express feelings appropriately and learn how to deal with situations that cause them. One approach is to hold the child till she calms down; another is to suggest an outlet that means something to her, perhaps running or listening to music or playing with clay. As adults, we sometimes release our anger by cleaning cupboards or jogging or sweeping the floor. Children need us to guide them in finding an outlet appropriate at their level.

The important thing is not to blame or punish a youngster for expressing his feelings. Instead of saying, "You are such a crybaby," why not try to find a reason for the crying and work on that. Say, perhaps, "I'd be unhappy, too, if those older boys wouldn't let me play in their game, so let's find something else to do that might be more fun." Suggest an option such as a game or activity the child likes, and play it with him for awhile.

It is also important to consider our child's needs before the views of others, or our own. We've all seen a small child have a tantrum in the grocery store. One customer may mutter disapprovingly while another may look on in sympathy, but whatever they think is unimportant. The main thing is to focus on our child and how to help him resolve the problem, not to focus on the looks or comments of others. And we should be prepared for our child to test the limits. When it comes to tantrums, setting limits and standing firm are essential. Tell the child that what he is doing is not safe, that he could hurt himself or others, or that it will damage property. Be consistent, and wait it out. There is nothing to be gained by worrying about the reflection on us, as parents. It may help to know that every parent has gone through it. In all likelihood, the main reaction of others is that they are glad that this time it is not their child acting out but someone else's!

Children aren't always able to sort out their emotions, and often they think they need permission to express them. If a child can't say he is happy or sad, life is confusing. We can begin by helping a child label his emotions, give them language. To a preschooler, for example, we might say, "I can see you're really angry." That validates the way the child feels and, in a sense, gives him permission to say how he feels. Then we can offer an option, or alternative. "It's not OK to hit your baby brother," you might say, "but you can use words. You can say, 'I'm mad.'" Wait for a calmer moment to talk to the child. Tell her that her feelings are OK, and show her some appropriate ways to handle her feelings.

Following are some useful tools for helping children—and ourselves—with our feelings and emotions.

- Listen actively. This means 1) identify the child's feelings, 2) acknowledge them, 3) sometimes do something about it, but sometimes just listen. It might help to reflect back to her: "You really had a crummy day." With older kids, we might ask how we can help them. For younger ones, we might offer a suggestion, then a hug. We shouldn't try to solve the problem. As more than one child has told his mother, "It's not your problem, mom."

- Try to trust in our children, to believe that, with guidance, they can handle their problems. Try to have a basic belief that children want to do well. Prepare for the worst, but expect the best. Look ahead; visualize a small goal: perhaps that our preschoolers will play peacefully for the next 10 minutes. Be realistic; don't expect them to play peacefully for the rest of the morning.

- Reinforce good behavior by telling our children when they are doing something well or especially nice. "You shared your toys so nicely with your little brother today," you might say, or "Thank you for being so polite to our guests this afternoon." However, when a correction does need to be made, resist the urge to criticize. Rather than scolding him for calling his little brother "dumb," suggest some nicer words he could use. It is easy to be critical, but it is more effective and helpful to reinforce good behavior.

- Recognize that feelings are OK, but some ways of expressing them are more appropriate than others. Take throwing a tantrum, for example. We can tell a child that it's OK to be mad: "I understand that you are angry (upset, whatever)." We should point out that yelling and screaming don't help a situation. Then we should offer some alternative options.

- When a child wants to talk, make the time for it. It might be late at night or when we are fixing dinner, but some things can't wait. If we keep putting off a child when he really wants to talk, he is likely to give up and find someone else who will listen. Parents who take time for their young children are far more likely to find their children willing to communicate when they are teenagers. The reverse also holds. If our teenagers don't communicate with us, it may be in part because we never encouraged them to develop a habit of communication.

- For a short time each day, give our child our complete attention. We might build into the day a minimum of five minutes per child, picking a time when neither parent nor child has things they want or have to do. We might find that we spend more time and enjoy it. But whether it is five minutes or more, each child will be able to look forward to his special time and we will both benefit by it.

- Learn to tolerate our own feelings and to handle them. It is something to work on daily and to model to our children consistently.

There are some things we should tell ourselves as parents. One is to set aside our own feelings of inadequacy or sense of guilt. Blaming parents for a child's misdeeds or problems is a common practice but neither a valid nor a fair one. Busy parents sometimes promise a child a special outing, then find that they can't keep the promise because of work demands or the baby is ill. Of course the child is disappointed; he wants his treat right now! And we, as parents, feel guilty that we have let the child down or angry that the child doesn't understand. It is best to apologize to the child and let him know why we couldn't keep the promise. It is also important to put aside our feelings of guilt for something that couldn't be helped.

If we feel stressed with our son or daughter, we need help to handle our stress rather than to try to change the child. Anyone who has ever had a child can understand how a parent can be at her wit's end, how a parent and child can both get upset or angry and lash out at the other, with the parent saying things she'll regret later or handing out punishment unrelated to the action. Instead, try to take a deep breath and problem solve through negotiation. For example, "When you did that, I really got angry. I really don't like that behavior. It could hurt someone." Sometimes that is enough. The child might even say he didn't know it could hurt you or make you angry. He might sulk and not admit a wrongdoing. Nevertheless, he might understand and be more careful next time. When both parent and child understand and the parent acts reasonably, the problem can be solved in a rational way. Unfair punishment makes children think that their parents want them to suffer because they made them angry, not because of their misbehavior.

An important part of the work of parenting is to prepare our children to grow into mentally and emotionally healthy human beings who can cope with and enjoy living in the adult world. One component is handling our feelings and being empathetic with the feelings of others. The younger children are when we teach them this, the easier it is for them to internalize. If they don't learn how to handle their own feelings and to understand the feelings of others, they are far more likely to have trouble developing relationships and getting along with others as they grow older.

Solving Problems and Tolerating Frustration

Have you ever seen a small child work diligently to put a jigsaw puzzle together, trying a piece in each open space until it fits, then starting all over again with another piece? Some children concentrate on a puzzle until they have put each piece in its proper place. On the other hand, some children might give up and walk away, some holler for mommy to come help them, and others become angry and scatter all the pieces before running off to do something else. Whatever each child's response, it would indicate not only his problem solving ability but also his ability to tolerate frustration.

The way in which a youngster masters a new toy is no different than the way in which she learns to ride a bike or play the piano, how he handles taking a test or playing on the soccer team, how she manages her first job or in time cares for her own infants. How a child develops an ability to solve problems and how well he learns to tolerate the frustration that comes from not mastering a task easily or quickly has an impact on him not only throughout his childhood but throughout his life.

Temperament is one thing that affects the way in which children tackle problems. Some children are easily agitated, some are more anxious, others fearful. For these children, the inability to complete a task with ease can be frustrating, leading to tears or anger. Children who are calm, take things in stride, or are highly motivated to succeed are more likely to tolerate frustration and, rather than get upset, complete their tasks.

For many parents, it is difficult to watch our children's frustration without stepping in to help. We generally want to fix things for our children, but it doesn't help to rush in to solve their problems.

Encouragement is important and helpful; taking over the solution is not. It is better to hold back when a child is struggling and to let him try to solve the problem. However, when a child is frustrated, try to empathize. Your toddler could be frustrated with a puzzle piece, and you could say, "That looks like a really hard puzzle." Your second grader could be struggling with math homework, and you could try, "It's difficult when you have so many numbers to add, isn't it?" This shows our child that we seem to understand what he is going through. On the other hand, if we say, "Oh, that's an easy one. You can do it," we might mean to be encouraging, but the child will find it deflating. By implication, what the child hears us say is that "it's easy so you must be dumb if you can't do it."

Children are quick to note how their parents work on problems and handle their own frustration. Have you ever been upset on Christmas Eve when you were trying to put a toy together, probably cussing at the confusing directions and swearing that one of the parts is missing? Most of us have. And what we modeled for our children is that (a) the problem is not our fault and (b) it is all right to get angry when something doesn't go right. Is that really the message we want to get across? Is that what we admire when we see other adults act in a similar manner? Not likely. It is certainly not the way to help our children learn to deal with things that don't go smoothly for them.

Children need guidance and encouragement, but they should be allowed to work the problem through. Trying to master the task at hand or solve a problem is a part of learning. Children, just as adults, learn through trial and error, through practice. They learn from small mistakes or failures and build on small successes. If our child doesn't do something perfectly—for example, the block tower she's building falls over, or he plays some wrong notes on a piano piece—we might tell them that each time they try they will do a bit better, then praise them for their efforts and for what they have accomplished.

It is best to encourage our children to hang in there rather than handling the situation for them. A child doesn't gain self-confidence if mom or dad completes his tasks for him. Rather, what the child learns is that he can get someone else to do his work. This doesn't mean we shouldn't help our children. Occasional suggestions and guidance are fine. However, completing a project may take time, and sometimes we just don't have the time to wait it out. To a young child we might say, "Mommy is in a hurry today, so let me help you finish that." Children can be very understanding as long as we don't use that excuse too often. It might be better to set up a time to work on the project later, "when I have time to work with you if you need help." This is reassuring for the child and saves ruffled feelings for both the child and his mother.

Tasks to be done and the decisions to be made should be age appropriate. Some projects become frustrating because they are too advanced or difficult for the child. It might help to break the project down into smaller tasks so a youngster can succeed at small steps along the way. And sometimes it is better to drop the project, putting it aside "until you are older" and substitute something with more potential for success. Self-confidence comes from accomplishment, from tackling real tasks and completing them successfully, from making decisions that work out well.

The same approach to solving problems of task completion applies to solving conflict. One approach is to ask our children for ideas about a solution. Take, for example, a mother who is at odds with her daughter about helping with household chores. Why not say something like, "I'm feeling overwhelmed and frustrated because I need help around the house. What do you think would help?" Or, when a preschooler and her friend want to play with the same toy, we might get ideas from each child on how to resolve the problem. Guide them, but don't solve the problem for them. Help them develop coping skills. Often young children need some direction, depending on their age and the situation, but they might surprise us with their creative and workable solutions.

Sometimes a parent can rephrase a problem for a youngster. The goal is to teach the child how to handle a situation, not just to tolerate it. For example, consider the following situation. Your young teenage daughter comes home in tears, hurt that the girls in her class snub her and don't let her eat lunch with them. What should a parent do? (a) Ask the teacher to intervene and tell the other girls to be friendlier. (b) Tell the daughter that it is probably not as bad as she thinks and to stop worrying about it. (c) Tell the girl that you've heard enough of that nonsense and stop talking about it. (d) Listen to the daughter, let her express her concerns in her own words, then guide her in possible ways to improve the situation, such as getting to know other girls with whom she might have more in common.

Now let's look at the answers: (a) Fixing the problem doesn't help the daughter learn how to handle her own problems. (b) Downplaying it denies the daughter's feelings. (c) Telling her to stop talking about it doesn't let the girl express her feelings or give her the support and help she is seeking. The best choice (d) provides the girl support when she is feeling down as well as helps her find a way to handle a difficult situation

In this era of instant gratification, some children experience another type of frustration, that of not getting what they want as soon as they want it. One reason is that today's parents, many of whom work long hours, often feel guilty because they have little time to spend with their children. Giving a child a new toy elicits a smile without effort, at least much less effort than giving time and attention would take. Offering gifts to make up for time not given is a type of emotional fast food and is of even less lasting value. Money and purchases can leave emptiness. They teach that friendship can be bought. It is an erroneous lesson.

One of the primary responsibilities of parents is to help children deal with frustrations and recognize that true gratification is rarely instant or effortless. There are ways to teach a child the value of delaying gratification and the joy that often follows. One mother gave her 10-year-old two options: she'd buy him sneakers for $30 right now, or she'd save for the $100 shoes he wanted by putting $30 away every month until enough was saved. "Then you can buy the expensive ones in June if you still want them," she said, "but not now." She was specific, for children that age are literal. She approached the problem at the child's developmental level and reasoned with him to reach a solution. The options were fair, with delay leading to an appropriate reward.

Accepting responsibility goes along with handling problems and tolerating frustration. This, too, is something to start at an early age. Getting up in the morning, getting their clothes on for school or play, and eating breakfast without too much dawdling are all things even very young children can do with just a little help and encouragement. Another is picking up toys before going to bed. With a two-year-old, we might say, "Now it's time to pick up our toys," then get down on the floor with the toddler and together start picking up and putting the blocks and trucks away. In time, with encouragement, he will probably start picking up the toys on his own. Being responsible helps build a child's feelings of self-worth. Everyone wants to be successful. For a two-year-old, picking up blocks is success. Often we feel that, as parents, everything is our responsibility. Why not let our children know that they are responsible, too.

Finally, we should recognize our own frustration or tolerance levels. When we parents are tired or overwhelmed and at the breaking point, when we are beyond acting reasonable, it helps to give ourselves a "time out." Perhaps both parent and child could go to different rooms for 10 minutes, or announce that "for the next 10 minutes, we'll each do something else, then we'll get back together to talk about the problem." In other words, suggest some option that gives everyone a chance to cool off. Or maybe your older daughter wants you to go with her to practice driving, but you've had a rough day and are in no mood to sit in the car with her as she lurches down the road. Rather than go with her and yell every time she does something wrong, why not acknowledge that it is not a good day for you. Don't blame her; just let her know that you will both have a better time if she will wait until later or the next day.

Getting Help

Sometimes, despite our best efforts, our children may need more help than we are able to give them. Perhaps our son can't seem to get along with other children or our daughter has seemed sad or depressed for too long a time. At this point, outside help might be called for. It is similar to when our youngster falls off a bike and hurts his arm. A responsible and concerned parent takes him to the doctor to see if his arm is broken and to get the proper treatment.

The same applies when a child is hurting emotionally. It is important to consult a mental health professional to determine if your child could benefit from counseling. Many cities have non-profit outpatient mental health centers, like the Austin Child Guidance Center, that specialize in services to children and that offer services on a sliding fee scale. There are also many excellent practitioners in private practice. Don't be afraid to ask questions before deciding upon where to take your child for help. You may want to first visit with the therapist before taking your child, to make sure he or she is someone with whom your family will be comfortable. Some questions to ask include how much experience he has working with children, special expertise in specific areas, and of course credentials and educational background as well as fees.

Conclusion

Just as most of us have not been trained to be parents, our children have come with no guarantees. Most of us do our best, confident at times but muddling along at other times, handling some situations well but knowing that we could have handled others better, happy and content with our children generally but concerned or distraught about them occasionally. And our children? All of them, even our cousin's perfect son and our neighbor's perfect daughter, have their good times and those not so good. They, too, travel an uneven road through life.

For some, the road is bumpier than for others; some children seem to get along better and find life easier than their peers, while others seem to bump heads constantly with other youngsters and irritate their elders. Perhaps this is due in part to inborn disposition, to the way they are wired. Perhaps it is due in part to environmental factors. Whatever the reasons, we as parents can do our best to help our children grow into mentally healthy young people and adults. With our guidance, our youngsters can travel the road to adulthood secure in the knowledge that they are loved, that they can get along with their family and peers, that they can face their problems and handle them, that they can recognize their emotions and express and deal with them appropriately, and that they can enjoy life and take pleasure in the people and activities around them. As long as we do our best to help our children develop these capabilities that are basic to good mental health, we will have fulfilled the aims and responsibilities that come with parenthood.

A Parent's Reminder

Birth to 18 months

Infants can't talk so they express themselves by crying, cooing, reaching for things. As they begin to crawl, then walk, and soon to talk, they get into things, often make a mess, don't always sleep when we think they should, scream when we're trying to hear someone talk, demand our attention when we have other things to do. Babies are cute and wonderful, yet they can be so time-consuming and irritating.

The Parent's Role

We can help our infants develop trust by meeting their needs for food, comfort, and protection. We can baby-proof the house for safety, yet give our infants freedom to move around and explore their world. We should never punish a baby by shaking or slapping or throwing down. Such action will make a baby fearful and may even cause permanent damage. Praise and encouragement work much better.

Most important—and hardest of all—is to be patient, calm, and consistent, even when we're irritated or exhausted or pushed to the limits. You're not alone; every parent is overstressed sometimes. Don't hold back love or comfort as a punishment, and try not to take out your frustration on your baby. Help your infant build trust through your consistent comfort and love.

18 months to 4 years

Toddlers try to become more independent by testing the limits, getting angry, and trying out new things such as pouring milk on the table or knocking over big brother's block tower. They begin to use words and soon become able to to express thoughts and ideas, ask "why" about everything, develop imagination through "pretend" play, and begin to understand the meaning of simple limits, such as not to touch a hot stove.

The Parent's Role

We can, and should, help our toddlers to become more independent by accepting their increasing skills and abilities, encouraging them to try new things, offering simple choices, giving short and clear instructions, and setting and enforcing limits and expectations. Again, it is important to be consistent. We should try not to be too demanding, not to set too many limits or say "no" too often, and not to use physical punishment, for toddlers can't understand the connection between their behavior and a spanking. We should avoid getting into power struggles with our children. Forcing toilet training or making a child clean his plate rarely works, and it usually leads to more problems. Growth is seldom smooth, but we're all happier if we can enjoy all the good experiences along the way.

4 to 6 years

As preschoolers develop, they initiate new ideas and activities, learn to share and cooperate, and seek approval by acting in ways they think are appropriate.

They may not always understand the difference between fantasy and reality, or wishes and lies. They tend to question everything, to compare differences between themselves and others, to spend less time with their parents and more with friends, to try to work out solutions to such preschool problems as how to keep a block tower from falling, and to begin sex role identification.

The Parent's Role

We can encourage initiative and simple problem solving by listening to our children and accepting their feelings, answering their questions honestly and fairly, and praising their efforts as well as their successes. It is important to set clear and reasonable limits and to give reasons for them, such as safety. Preschoolers need help and reassurance with problem solving, with learning the difference between fact and fantasy. We should try not to create guilt in our preschoolers by shaming, lecturing, criticizing, or teasing. We wouldn't like that, and neither would they.

6 to 12 years

When children reach school age, they try out and test their abilities, skills, and talents. They become more competitive, get interested in group activities, learn sportsmanship. They develop close friendships, mostly with the same sex, and do more activities independently from their parents. They begin to learn the importance of completing tasks, and of working both independently and with others, such as in a school project or group activity.

The Parent's Role

The best ways to encourage skill development and independent growth are to support and praise our youngsters' talents, achievements, and accomplishments. As they become more independent, it is important to help them develop sound values, to learn right from wrong, to make considered choices. Rules are necessary, and we should give reasons for them. We should also listen to our children, talk with them about problems and solutions. We should encourage them to complete their tasks or assignments and help them learn to set priorities. Praise and encouragement are key words here. If we put down children's ideas or ambitions, it may discourage them from trying; if we shame them or make them feel guilty, it will discourage them from talking to or listening to us. Positive reinforcement is far more likely to lead to positive growth and behavior.

12 to 18 years

Adolescence can be a turbulent time, with physical changes, emotional and mood swings, strong opinions, and often a seeming lack of respect for parental values and concerns. It is a time of increasing learning and skill development and learning to handle responsibilities. It is also a time of testing parental limits, of insecurity and doubt that often masquerades as self-confidence. They are developing autonomy, preparing to separate from their parents. Adolescents want to belong; friends, clubs and teams seem more important to them than family. They have to make choices about things that matter, such as drugs, sex, and friends, and because they want to belong or are unsure of themselves, they sometimes make poor choices. Luckily, most youngsters live through adolescence, growing and in time becoming self-accepting and more accepting of their parents.

The Parent's Role

Difficult as it may be, parents can encourage personal growth and independence by being patient with their adolescents, patient with their moods and demands and not offended by their criticism. Teenagers need room to grow, to learn from their mistakes as well as from their successes. It is important, however, to stick to rules, to be consistent but fair. Even though they may look like adults and consider themselves grown, it is essential to continue to offer them guidance and support. With guidance, teenagers can learn to use their consciences, set positive goals, develop values, and make good decisions for themselves.

Adolescents also need accurate sexual information. Sex plays an increasingly dominant role throughout the teen years.

The teenage years can be difficult for teens and parents alike. However stressed or upset we may be, we should never label our teens as impossible or hopeless. We shouldn't reject them when they push the limits or criticize them if they express beliefs or opinions that differ from our own. Discipline may be called for, but we should try to avoid discipline that is too harsh or inappropriate. Patience, understanding, and fairness can go a long way in helping our teens, and ourselves.

All Ages

Despite our best efforts, problems tend to arise, problems that we are unsure how to resolve or are more than we can handle alone. Fortunately, there are resources to help families work out their problems. Among them is the Austin Child Guidance Center. The center's professional staff is trained to help with many of these problems or to refer you to an agency that can. The earlier that families recognize the need for assistance, the better the outcome.

About the Author

Louise K. Iscoe has had a long career writing and editing for The University of Texas, Southwest Texas State University, the Hogg Foundation for Mental Health, and state agencies, focusing primarily on early childhood, education, and the social sciences. Among her publications are two books: *Ima Hogg, First Lady of Texas* and *Overcoming: A History of Black Integration at The University of Texas*, and a number of booklets on The School of the Future, a multi-million dollar school-based health and human services project funded by the Hogg Foundation.

About the Illustrator

Carl Pickhardt, Ph.D. is an author, graphic artist, and psychologist in private counseling and lecturing practice in Austin, Texas. For information about his books and to read his monthly articles about parenting and family relationships, visit his website: *www.carlpickhardt.com.*

About the Center

Austin Child Guidance Center is committed to improving the mental health of children through parent education, evaluation, and counseling for children and families. One in five youth experience emotional or behavioral problems which can lead to conflict at home, rejection by peers and difficulties or failure at school. The Center has helped thousands of children (and their parents) with attention deficit hyperactivity disorder (ADHD), parent/child communication difficulties, trauma related to violence or abuse, depression, and anxiety, as well as those coping with major family crisis and divorce.

About the Cover

Art Director Beth Fowler evokes the vibrancy of parenting in her cover design by combining children's primary colors with adult black and white line art. An author/illustrator published by Simon & Schuster, BrownTrout and St. David's Press, she creates her *In the Weeds*® greeting cards in Austin.

How You Can Help

The Center, which began providing services in 1951, is a private, non-profit 501(c)3 corporation. Fees are based on income and size of family, and no family is denied services based on inability to pay. Funding from United Way/Capital Area, City of Austin and Travis County support this sliding fee scale, and a variety of special programs are funded by other sources. Donations increase the ability to see low-income clients and are welcomed. For more information about the Center, please visit *www.austinchildguidance.org*

Principles of Good Parenting
Order Form

To send a book to a friend or to get another copy for
yourself, just fill out the form below, enclose a check
or money order for the total ($9.95 per book;
$8.45 for 10-50 books; $7.95 for 51 or more),
and send it to:

Austin Child Guidance Center
810 West 45th St., Austin, TX 78751
512-451-2242

Qty.	Description	Price	Extended Price
	Principles of Good Parenting	$	$
Shipping & Handling ($2.00/book; $1.00 for 10 or more)			$
		Total	$

Recipient Information:

Name:

Address:

City: State   Zip Code

Phone:

Email: